the guide to owning a
Cavalier King Charles Spaniel

Stacy Kennedy

T.F.H. Publications, Inc.
One TFH Plaza
Third and Union Avenues
Neptune City, NJ 07753

This book has been published with the intent to provide accurate and authoritative information in regard to the subject matter within. While every precaution has been taken in preparation of this book, the publisher and author assume no responsibility for errors or omissions. Neither is any liability assumed for damages resulting from the use of the information herein.

ISBN 0-7938-1901-6

www.tfh.com

Contents

The History of the Cavalier King Charles Spaniel

If you've ever examined any of the 16th-, 17th-, and 18th-century paintings by Titian, Gainsborough, Reynolds, Landseer, Van Dyck, Lely, Romney, or Stubbs, then you've observed the ancestors of today's Cavalier King Charles Spaniels. These works of art feature a small spaniel

Originally a sporting dog, the Cavalier King Charles Spaniel became a favorite of the gentry of the day.

The AKC first recognized the Cavalier King Charles Spaniel in 1994. Two years later, the breed became eligible for championship points as a member of the Toy Group.

THE GUIDE TO OWNING A CAVALIER KING CHARLES SPANIEL

The Cavalier comes in four acceptable colors: blenheim, tricolor, black and tan, and ruby.

with a flat head, high-set ears, almond eyes, and a pointed nose, and demonstrate that the Cavalier charm has been around for ages. During Tudor times, these Toy Spaniels were quite common as ladies' lap dogs; however, they reached the height of popularity during the reign of King Charles II, who was seldom seen without two or three of the animals. In fact, King Charles II was so enamored of his dogs that he wrote a decree proclaiming that the breed should be accepted in any public place, even in the Houses of Parliament.

In the early days of England, dog shows and recognized breed standards did not exist, so both type and size of the early Cavalier dogs varied. By the mid-19th century, the English began to take dog breeding and showing more seriously. The Toy Spaniel subsequently evolved with a completely flat face, undershot jaw, domed skull with long, low set ears, and large, round eyes, making the King Charles Spaniel as depicted in early paintings virtually extinct.

An American by the name of Roswell Eldridge began to search for Toy Spaniels in England that resembled those in the old paintings, including a painting by Sir Edwin Landseer entitled "The Cavalier's Dogs," but the only dogs he could find were the short-faced "Charlies." In 1926, Eldridge persuaded The Kennel Club to allow him to offer prizes at Crufts Dog Show for the dogs of the Blenheim variety as seen during King

Charles II's reign—25 pounds sterling for the best dog and 25 pounds sterling for the best bitch.

Unfortunately, Roswell Eldridge died at age 70, only a month before the 1928 Crufts show, where "Ann's Son," a dog owned by Miss Mostyn Walker, was awarded the prize. In that same year, a breed club was founded and the name "Cavalier King Charles Spaniel" chosen.

At the breed club's first meeting, held the second day of Crufts in 1928, the standard of the breed was drawn up, which remains almost the same today. Ann's Son was designated as an example, and it was agreed that the Cavalier should be a perfectly natural dog with no trimming. In 1945, The Kennel Club granted the breed separate registration and awarded Challenge Certificates in order to allow the Cavalier King Charles Spaniel to compete and gain championship titles.

CAVALIERS IN THE US

Around this time in the US, Mrs. W.L. Lyons Brown of Kentucky brought a Cavalier home from England. She found others in America who owned Cavaliers and, in 1956, she organized the CKCSC-USA. The group gathered in Prospect, Kentucky in the early 1960s for the first ever Cavalier King Charles Spaniel Specialty Show in America. By that time, 118 dogs had been registered, with 68 of them born in the US of 24 litters. To this day, the CKCSC-USA keeps complete records of litters, imported Cavaliers, stud books, etc., in addition to organizing specialty shows around the country. In 1985, the CKCSC-USA held a Silver Jubilee Show in Prospect, Kentucky, marking the 25th consecutive CKCSC-USA Specialty show.

Under pressure by the American Kennel Club to move the breed out of the Miscellaneous Class, the Cavalier fancy split into two national breed clubs in 1995. The Cavalier became fully recognized by the AKC in January of 1996. The original CKCSC-USA has repeatedly voted against recognition by the AKC and declined the offer to be the AKC-recognized national breed club. The American Cavalier King Charles Spaniel Club (ACKCSC) was subsequently formed, recognized by the AKC, and wrote the current AKC standard.

The Standard for the Cavalier King Charles Spaniel

General Appearance—The Cavalier King Charles Spaniel is an active, graceful, well-balanced toy spaniel, very gay and free in action; fearless and sporting in character, yet at the same time gentle and affectionate. It is this typical gay temperament, combined with true elegance and royal

Becoming familiar with the breed standard will make choosing the right Cavalier King Charles Spaniel for your family easier.

The Cavalier King Charles Spaniel is an active, graceful, well-balanced toy spaniel that is fearless and sporting in character, yet at the same time gentle and affectionate.

appearance which are of paramount importance in the breed. Natural appearance with no trimming, sculpting or artificial alteration is essential to breed type.

Size, Proportion, Substance— *Size*—Height 12 to 13 inches at the withers; weight proportionate to height, between 13 and 18 pounds. A small, well balanced dog within these weights is desirable, but these are ideal heights and weights and slight variations are permissible. *Proportion*—The body approaches squareness, yet if measured from point of shoulder to point of buttock, is slightly longer than the height at the withers. The height from the withers to the elbow is approximately equal to the height from the elbow to the ground. *Substance*—Bone moderate in proportion to size. Weedy and coarse specimens are to be equally penalized.

Head—Proportionate to size of dog, appearing neither too large nor too small for the body. *Expression*—The sweet, gentle, melting expression is an important breed characteristic. *Eyes*—Large, round, but not prominent and set well apart; color a warm, very dark brown; giving a lustrous, limpid look. Rims dark. There should be cushioning under the eyes which contributes to the soft expression. *Faults*—small, almond-shaped, prominent, or light eyes; white surrounding ring. *Ears*—

The Cavalier's coat should be of moderate length, silky, and free from curl. A slight wave is permitted.

Your Cavalier need to get used to having his teeth checked if you plan on showing him. The Cavalier's bite should be a perfect, regular, and complete scissor bite.

THE GUIDE TO OWNING A CAVALIER KING CHARLES SPANIEL

Set high, but not close, on top of the head. Leather long with plenty of feathering and wide enough so that when the dog is alert, the ears fan slightly forward to frame the face. *Skull*—Slightly rounded, but without dome or peak; it should appear flat because of the high placement of the ears. Stop is moderate, neither filled nor deep. *Muzzle*—Full muzzle slightly tapered. Length from base of stop to tip of nose about 1 1/2 inches. Face well filled below eyes. Any tendency towards snipiness undesirable. Nose pigment uniformly black without flesh marks and nostrils well developed. *Lips* well developed but not pendulous giving a clean finish. *Faults*—Sharp or pointed muzzles. *Bite*—A perfect, regular and complete scissors bite is preferred, i.e. the upper teeth closely overlapping the lower teeth and set square into the jaws. *Faults*—undershot bite, weak or crooked teeth, crooked jaws.

Neck, Topline, Body—*Neck*—Fairly long, without throatiness, well enough muscled to form a slight arch at the crest. Set smoothly into nicely sloping shoulders to give an elegant look. *Topline*—Level both when moving and standing. *Body*—Short-coupled with ribs well spring but not barrelled. Chest moderately deep, extending to elbows allowing ample heart room. Slightly less body at the flank than at the last rib, but with no tucked-up appearance. *Tail*—Well set on, carried happily but never much above the level of the back, and in constant characteristic motion when the dog is in action. Docking is optional. If docked, no more than one third to be removed.

Forequarters—*Shoulders* well laid back. *Forelegs* straight and well under the dog with elbows close to the sides. *Pasterns* strong and feet compact with well-cushioned pads. Dewclaws may be removed.

Hindquarters—The hindquarters construction should come down from a good broad pelvis, moderately muscled; stifles well turned and hocks well let down. The hindlegs when viewed from the rear should parallel each other from hock to heel. *Faults*—Cow or sickle hocks.

Coat—Of moderate length, silky, free from curl. Slight wave permissible. Feathering on ears, chest, legs and tail should be long, and the feathering on the feet is a feature of the breed. No trimming of the dog is permitted. *Specimens where the coat has been altered by trimming, clipping, or by artificial means shall be so severely penalized as to be effectively eliminated from competition.* Hair growing between the pads on the underside of the feet may be trimmed.

Color—*Blenheim*—Rich chestnut markings well broken up on a clear, pearly white ground. The ears must be chestnut and the color evenly spaced on the head and surrounding both eyes, with a white blaze between the eyes and ears, in the center of which may be the lozenge or "Blenheim spot". The lozenge is a unique and desirable, though not essential, characteristic of the Blenheim. *Tricolor*—Jet black markings well broken up on a clear, pearly white ground. The ears must be black and the color evenly spaced on the head and surrounding both eyes, with a white blaze between the eyes. Rich tan markings over the eyes, on cheeks, inside ears and on underside of tail. *Ruby*—Whole-colored rich red. *Black and Tan*—Jet black with rich, bright tan markings over eyes, on cheeks, inside ears, on chest, legs, and on underside of tail. *Faults*—Heavy ticking on Blenheims or Tricolors, white marks on Rubies or Black and Tans.

Gait—Free moving and elegant in action, with good reach in front and sound, driving rear action. When viewed from the side, the movement exhibits a good length of stride, and viewed from front and rear it is straight and true, resulting from straight-boned fronts and properly made and muscled hindquarters.

Temperament—Gay, friendly, non-aggressive with no tendency towards nervousness or shyness. *Bad temper, shyness, and meanness are not to be tolerated and are to be severely penalized as to effectively remove the specimen from competition.*

Approved Date: January 10, 1995
Effective Date: April 30, 1995

Selecting Your Cavalier King Charles Spaniel

The purchase of any dog, especially the Cavalier King Charles Spaniel, is an important step, because the well-cared-for Cavalier will live with you for many years. Once the prospective Cavalier King Charles Spaniel owner decides that he is definitely ready for the responsibilities of dog ownership,

There are many things to consider when selecting your new Cavalier King Charles Spaniel. Take your time and never rush into a decision.

he will undoubtedly want to rush out and purchase a puppy right away. This is not a good idea, since it is extremely important that anyone considering taking home a Cavalier King Charles Spaniel thoroughly researches the breed. The Cavalier King Charles Spaniel is not the breed for everyone; this dog will require lots of time, attention, and training, as well as plenty of outdoor activity. You must be certain that a Cavalier King Charles Spaniel will fit in with your family, home environment, and lifestyle.

FINDING A GOOD BREEDER

It is very important that you purchase your Cavalier King Charles Spaniel from a breeder who has earned a reputation for consistently producing dogs that are physically healthy and mentally sound. Breeders earn a reputation for quality by selectively breeding their dogs. Selective breeding aims to maintain the virtues of a breed and eliminate genetic weaknesses. The American Kennel Club or the American Cavalier King Charles Spaniel Club can assist a prospective dog buyer in finding a responsible breeder of quality stock.

The responsible Cavalier King Charles Spaniel breeder will breed for good temperament over any other characteristic and will ensure that his puppies are properly socialized. The socialization process should not be overlooked, as proper socialization will help produce a mentally stable dog able to get along with all kinds of people and other animals. A well-socialized Cavalier King Charles Spaniel will not exhibit fear, shyness, or aggressiveness. Because Cavalier King Charles Spaniel pups need human contact right from the beginning, it is important that the breeder spends a lot of time with each puppy individually to establish the human/canine relationship.

With any luck, you will find a reputable breeder residing in your area who will not only provide the right Cavalier King Charles Spaniel for you, but will have the parents of the puppy on the premises as well. Meeting the puppy's parents will give you the opportunity to observe the quality of his lineage firsthand. The Cavalier's parents should be certified with the Orthopedic Foundation for Animals (OFA) as free of hip dysplasia and the Canine Eye Registration Foundation (CERF) as free of hereditary eye diseases such as cataracts and progressive retinal atrophy. Good breeders are not only willing to allow you to see the dam (mother) and sire (father) of the litter, but also to inspect the facility in which the dogs are raised. Additionally these breeders will readily discuss with you any genetic problems that exist in the breed, explain how these problems are dealt with, and demonstrate which measures are employed to safeguard against them.

Visit several different breeders before making your decision. Ask plenty of questions and be prepared to answer some as well.

Do not be surprised if a concerned breeder asks lots of questions about you, your family, and the environment in which your Cavalier King Charles Spaniel will be raised. Responsible breeders are just as concerned that their dogs are going to good homes as you, the buyer, are in obtaining a well-adjusted, healthy dog. The breeder will use all of the information you give him to match the right puppy with the right home. For example, a quiet, single adult generally requires a puppy with a different personality than the dog that is appropriate for a household full of young, energetic children. The new owner of a Cavalier King Charles Spaniel should be able to provide him with the exercise and positive outlets that this breed requires. The time you spend in making the right selection ensures that you will obtain the right dog for your lifestyle.

If there are no local breeders in your area, legitimate and reliable breeders are located throughout the country; they will appear on the American Cavalier King Charles Spaniel Club or national kennel club lists. These established breeders safely ship puppies to different states and even different countries. Always check the references of these breeders and do not hesitate to ask for documentation as well. The breeder will undoubtedly have as many questions for you as you will have for him or her. Communicating as much information as you can to the breeder will ensure that you go home with the pup with the temperament best suited for you.

When arriving at the breeder's home or kennel, the buyer should look for cleanliness in both the dogs and the areas in which they are kept. In fact, the cleanliness of the dogs and the condition of the area in which they sleep and play strongly indicate how well the breeder treats his puppies.

A healthy little Cavalier King Charles Spaniel puppy should feel strong and sturdy to the touch, neither too thin nor obese and bloated. The coat should be shiny and clean, with no sign of dry or flaky skin. The puppy's eyes should be clear, bright, and free of redness or irritation. It's important that the inside of the puppy's ears be pink—discharge or a bad odor could indicate ear mites or infection. A pup that coughs, has diarrhea, or has any eruptions on the skin is usually ill and should not be considered. In fact, if one puppy shows signs of illness, the health of the whole litter must be questioned.

As you are making a commitment to the puppy for his lifetime, make sure he reacts positively toward you and members of your family. Select the puppy that seems outgoing and ready to trust you. Sit down with the puppies and see which one is interested in playing. If you are looking for strictly a companion pet, pick the puppy that wants to be with you and enjoys your company. Take the puppy you are interested in away from his littermates into another room or another part of the kennel. The smells will remain the same for the puppy, so he should still feel secure and maintain his personality, but this isolation technique will allow you to inspect the puppy more closely and without distractions. If the puppy ignores you or seems more interested in going back to his littermates, choose another one.

Most breeders will not allow their puppies to go home with their new owners until after they have been received their first vaccinations—usually at about seven weeks of age. Once weaned, your pup is highly susceptible to many infectious diseases that can be transmitted through people. It is best to make sure your Cavalier is fully inoculated before he leaves the breeder's residence, and you should continue his immunization schedule with your veterinarian.

When you finally purchase your Cavalier King Charles Spaniel, remember that the purchase of any purebred dog entitles you to three very important documents: a copy of the dog's pedigree, a health record containing an inoculation schedule, and the dog's registration certificate.

HEALTH RECORD

The breeder from whom you buy your Cavalier King Charles Spaniel puppy should have initiated the necessary inoculation series for the litter by

Puppies need lots of attention when they first arrive into your home. If your time is limited, consider adopting an adult Cavalier instead. Ask your veterinarian about local shelters or rescue organizations.

the time the puppies are eight weeks of age. These inoculations protect them against hepatitis, leptospirosis, distemper, and canine parvovirus. In most cases, rabies inoculations are not given until a puppy is four months of age or older.

These inoculations are given as a series and it is very important that your Cavalier King Charles Spaniel puppy receives the full set in order for them to be effective. The veterinarian you choose will then be able to continue on an appropriate inoculation schedule.

PEDIGREE

The breeder must supply you with a copy of your Cavalier King Charles Spaniel's pedigree, a document that authenticates your puppy's ancestors back to at least the third generation. All purebred dogs have a pedigree. The pedigree does not imply that a dog is of show quality, but simply provides a chronological list of ancestors. The pedigree may be helpful in determining if your Cavalier King Charles Spaniel's relatives have any titles in obedience or field trials, which can then indicate the trainability and work ethic of the pup's parents and grandparents.

REGISTRATION CERTIFICATE

A country's governing kennel club issues the registration certificate. When you transfer the ownership of your Cavalier King Charles Spaniel from the breeder's name to your own name, the transaction is entered on this certificate. When mailed to the kennel club, the registration certificate is then permanently recorded in its files. You will need to produce this document if you decide to show your Cavalier King Charles Spaniel.

DIET

Most breeders will give the new owner a written record that details the amount and kind of food a puppy has been eating. Follow these recommendations exactly, at least for the first month or two after the puppy comes to live with you. The instructions should indicate the number of times a day your puppy has been fed and the kind of vitamin supplementation he has been receiving, if any. If you follow the breeder's instructions, the chance of your Cavalier King Charles Spaniel puppy suffering from an upset stomach and diarrhea will be greatly reduced.

The breeder's diet sheet should project the increases and changes in food that will be necessary as your puppy grows from week to week. If the breeder does not provide you with this information, ask your veterinarian for suggestions. If and when you decide to change the type or brand of dog food you are giving your Cavalier King Charles Spaniel, do so gradually, mixing the old food with the new until the substitution is completed.

A dog that has been sociaized from an early age will be a delight to have around.

HEALTH GUARANTEE

Any reputable breeder will be more than willing to supply a written agreement that the puppy you choose to take home must be able to pass a veterinarian's examination. Furthermore, the puppy should be guaranteed against the development of any hereditary problems. You should choose a veterinarian before deciding on your Cavalier King Charles Spaniel and arrange an appointment with him right after you have picked up your puppy from the breeder and before you take the puppy home. If this is not possible, you should not delay this procedure any longer than 24 hours after the puppy leaves the breeder's residence.

SOCIALIZATION

A Cavalier King Charles Spaniel's temperament is both hereditary and learned. A Cavalier King Charles Spaniel pup can inherit a bad temperament from one or both of his parents; a bad-tempered disposition will definitely not make a good pet or working dog. A poor temperament can also be caused by a lack of socialization or mistreatment. The first step in obtaining a stable and well-adjusted companion is to choose a happy puppy from a breeder who is determined to produce good temperaments and has taken all the necessary steps to provide early socialization. Your puppy should stay with his dam and littermates until at least seven weeks of age, because the interaction with them will help your Cavalier King Charles Spaniel get along with other dogs later in life.

Once you bring your Cavalier King Charles Spaniel puppy home, it is necessary to continue the socialization begun by the breeder. You should introduce your Cavalier King Charles Spaniel puppy to everyone, especially children. If you have young children in your family, teach them to treat the puppy with respect. If you do not have children, find some gentle playmates to romp with your puppy. Energetic children make wonderful playmates for the energetic Cavalier King Charles Spaniel—and vice versa.

Take the puppy to as many different environments as you can—the beach, the park, the store, and the car. Expose him to different noises and situations, such as busy streets or crowded pet stores, always on lead, of course. Introduce him to other well-socialized dogs. All Cavalier King Charles Spaniels must learn to get along with other dogs as well as with humans. Find a "puppy kindergarten" class in your area and attend regular-ly. Not only is it a great place to socialize you dog, it is also the first step in training the new addition to your family.

RESCUE CAVALIERS

Although they mostly deal with adult dogs, a purebred rescue organization can be a good place to find a Cavalier. Run by volunteers, the American Cavalier King Charles Spaniel Club sponsors rescue groups that help place dogs into new homes. Most of them work in conjunction with animal shelters, which alert the rescue organization if a purebred dog is brought in. The volunteers will provide foster homes for the dogs, assess their health and temperament, screen them for training and social skills, and care for the dogs until new homes are found for them.

As mentioned before, most of the dogs fostered in rescue groups are adults, but you can call and ask to be put on the waiting list for a puppy. You can get in touch with a breed rescue group in your area by calling the local humane society or the AKC, both of which maintain a list of national breed rescue coordinators.

Feeding Your Cavalier King Charles Spaniel

Good nutrition is a necessary requirement in your Cavalier King Charles Spaniel's life. Providing your dog with the proper diet is one of the most important aspects of caring for him. By carefully researching which diet is the best one, you can ensure his good health, which will affect all other parts of your life together.

Your Cavalier King Charles Spaniel needs a highly nutritious dog food to stay healthy. The amount of food and the number of feedings daily will vary depending on your dog's age.

DOG FOODS

If you take a trip to your local pet emporium or supermarket, you cannot help but notice that there is an overwhelming selection of dog foods available. The variety can be confusing, to say the least, and this makes it hard to choose which brand is best for your Cavalier. There are certain things you should know about commercial dog food that will help you make the right decision. The more you educate yourself about what your dog's nutritional needs are, the easier the decision will be.

In order to stay healthy, there are six essential nutrients that all dogs in every stage of life require in varied amounts: protein, fat, carbohydrates, vitamins, minerals, and water.

Protein

Protein may be burned as calories, stored as fat, and can help with muscle growth, tissue repair, blood clotting, and immunity functions. Good sources of protein are meat, fish, poultry, milk, cheese, yogurt, fish-meal, and eggs.

Fat

Fat supplies the energy needed for the absorption of certain vitamins, provides insulation from cold, and makes food tastier. Fat can be found in meat and meat by-products and vegetable oils, such as safflower, olive, corn, and soybean.

Carbohydrates

Carbohydrates provide energy and keep intestines functioning smoothly. Complex carbohydrates are comprised of fiber and sugar and can be found in corn, oats, wheat, rice, and barley.

Vitamins

Vitamins are divided into two groups—water soluble and fat soluble. Different vitamins have different functions: vitamin A protects skin and promotes bone growth, vitamin B aids in metabolism, vitamin D aids in bone growth and increases calcium absorption, and vitamin K helps with blood clotting. Good sources of vitamins are fruit, vegetables, cereals, and the livers of most animals.

Minerals

Minerals provide strength to bone and ensure proper bone formation, maintain fluid balance and normal muscle and nerve function, transport oxygen to the blood, and produce hormones. Examples of minerals are calcium, phosphorus, copper, iron, magnesium, selenium, potassium, zinc, and sodium.

Water

The most important of all nutrients, water makes up over 60 percent of a dog. Water intake can come directly through drinking or can be released when food is oxidized. If your dog's diet is lacking in water, dehydration can occur, which can lead to serious breakdown of organs or even death. All dogs must retain a water balance, which means that their total intake of

Puppies need plenty of fresh, clear water to remain healthy. Water should be available at all times, especially during mealtime and after exercise.

water should be in balance with the total output. Make sure that your puppy has access to cool, clean water at all times.

TYPES OF DOG FOOD

First, you should pick a dog food that is specially formulated for active dogs. This will ensure that your Cavalier King Charles Spaniel is getting the proper nutrition for growth and digestion for his undeveloped systems. There are three types of dog food available on the market today, and all of them have good and bad points. You must choose the type that best fits you and your puppy's needs.

Dry Food

The good thing about dry food is that it is the least expensive, can conveniently be left in bowl for longer periods of time, and helps control tartar. However, it is the least appealing to dogs.

Canned food

Canned food is the most appealing to dogs, but it spoils quickly, is the most expensive, and requires more to be fed because the energy content is relatively low, especially for large or active breeds.

Semi-Moist

Semi-moist food will not spoil at room temperature and comes in prepackaged servings, but it also contains large amounts of sugar and preservatives in order to remain fresh without refrigeration.

READING LABELS

There are two agencies that work together in regulating pet food labels. The first agency, the Association of American Feed Control Officials (AAFCO), is a non-governmental agency made up of state and federal officials from around the United States. They establish pet food regulations that cover areas like guaranteed analysis, nutritional adequacy statements, and feeding directions. Each state decides whether or not to enforce AAFCO's regulations. Most do; however, some do not.

The second agency, the Food and Drug Administration Center for Veterinary Medicine, establishes and enforces standards for all animal feed. This federal agency oversees aspects of labeling that cover proper identification of products, net quantity statements, and the list of ingredients.

Learn how to read dog food labels, especially when you consider how many brands are out there. Slight changes in wording can make the difference between a quality dog food and one that may not appear to be what it seems.

PRODUCT NAME

You may think the name of your dog food is just a name, but in most cases that name can make a big difference. Specific words used in the name can indicate what is in the food and what is not. For example, a brand name like "Beef Dog Food" must contain at least 95 percent beef, but if it is called "Beef *Formula* for Dogs," it is required to contain a minimum of only 25 percent beef. Other words like dinner, platter, nuggets, and entrée fall under this 25 percent minimum requirement.

Another word to watch for is "with." A dog food called "Dog Food with Beef" only has to contain a minimum of 3 percent beef. The word "with" was originally supposed to highlight extra ingredients, but recent amendments to AAFCO regulations now allow the word to be used in the product's name. Also, the word "flavored" can be deceiving, because it means that only a sufficient amount of flavoring needs to be added for it to be detectable. Therefore. "Beef Flavored Dog Food" may not include any beef at all and may only be flavored with very small amounts of beef by-products.

INGREDIENT LIST

Each ingredient contained in the dog food will be listed in descending order according to weight. However, the quality of each ingredient is not required to be listed. For best results, look for animal-based proteins to be high up on the list, and include beef,

beef by-products, chicken, chicken by-products, lamb, lamb meal, fish meal, and egg. However, use caution and read carefully, because some manufacturers will manipulate the weight of products in order to place it higher or lower on the list. For example, they may divide the grains into different categories, like wheat flour and whole ground wheat, in order to lower the weight and make it seem less prominent on the ingredient list.

You may be wondering what exactly meat by-products and meal are, anyway. Actual "meat" is considered to be the clean flesh of a slaughtered mammal and is limited to the part of the striate muscle that is skeletal or found in the tongue, diaphragm, heart, or esophagus. Meat by-products are the non-rendered lean parts other than the meat, which include, but are not limited to, the lungs, spleen, kidney, bone, blood, stomach, intestines, necks, feet, and undeveloped eggs. Meat and bone meal are the rendered product or mammal tissue, which include bone, hair hood, horn, hide trimming, manure, and stomach. As you can see, the ingredients in dog food can vary widely, so be informed as to what your puppy is actually eating.

GUARANTEED ANALYSIS
The guaranteed analysis states the minimum amount of crude protein and crude fat as well as the maximum amount percentage of moisture (water) and crude fiber. The word "crude" refers to the method of testing the product, not the quality of the nutrient. Sometimes manufactures will list other nutrients like ash or calcium, although they are not required to do so.

NUTRITIONAL ADEQUACY STATEMENT
The nutritional adequacy statement is important when looking for a dog food for puppies because it states what life stage the product is formulated for, such as growth, reproduction, maintenance, senior, or all life stages. For developing puppies, look for the product that is specially formulated for growth. It should also tell you whether the product is "complete and balanced" or "complementary." Complete and balanced means that it contains all the ingredients your dog will need on a daily basis and that it can be served by itself. Complementary means that it is not intended to be used alone and must be added to another product to create a complete meal.

NET QUANTITY STATEMENT
The net quality statement shows the weight of the food in the bag or can in pounds and ounces as well as metric weight. Be careful, because some companies use 30-pound bags and then only put 25 pounds of food inside.

FEEDING INSTRUCTIONS

The feeding instructions on a dog food label are only suggestions; some dogs will eat more, some less. Also, these instructions provide the amounts needed for the entire day, so you can divide it up the best way for you and your puppy. If you are not sure how much to feed your dog, start off with the suggested amount and increase or decrease as necessary.

Although dog food labels tell you a lot about a product, there is a lot that they don't tell you. For example, some wording used on labels can be misleading. Foods that use the words "gourmet" or "premium" are not required to contain any higher quality ingredients than any other product. Products that claim to be "all-natural" are not required to be. Some might think that this means the food is minimally processed or contains no artificial ingredients, but this is not necessarily true. In fact, all dog foods must contain some chemically synthesized ingredients in order to be deemed complete and balanced.

HOMEMADE DIETS

There seems to be a debate about whether a homemade diet is better for your dog than manufactured dog food. The downside to feeding a homemade diet is that you need to be very careful to ensure you are providing your puppy with all of the necessary nutrients. It also takes a lot of time, effort, and energy to cook a proper diet for your dog on a daily basis.

Those in favor of a homemade diet believe that commercial dog foods contain contaminated and unhealthy ingredients and feel that it is worth the effort to give their puppy a home-cooked meal. If you have the time and money and believe it is important to feed your puppy a homemade diet, consult your veterinarian, who can give you a reputable and nutritionally balanced recipe. Although millions of dogs remains healthy on commercially prepared dog food, the ultimate decision is yours.

Now that you have learned all you can about dog food and feeding options, you can make an informed choice about what to buy for your puppy.

FEEDING YOUR CAVALIER KING CHARLES SPANIEL PUPPY

If you are lucky, the breeder from whom you obtained your Cavalier King Charles Spaniel will have given you a diet sheet which will help you immensely with your feeding chores. A diet sheet will typically tell you the type of food your puppy has been eating, when he eats, and how to increase his food intake as he ages. Some breeders will even include enough food to get you through a day or two. If possible, follow this original feeding schedule as closely as possible and use

A feeding schedule will help to make sure that your dog is being fed the proper amount of food each day.

the same brand of puppy food for the first few months. This will help avoid any stomach upsets or diarrhea. If you would like to change the brand of food your puppy is eating, do so gradually, slowly mixing the old food with the new food over a period of time until the old food is totally replaced.

If no diet sheet was provided for you, you will have to use the information available about dog food and choose one that is specially formulated for puppies. It should indicate that it is a growth formula as well. If you are undecided about which brand to choose, consult your veterinarian.

How will you know if you have made the right choice? First, take a look at your puppy's stool. It should be small and firm, neither too loose nor too dry. A large amount of stool means the food is not being digested. Although it may take a few months to notice, a puppy eating a nutritious diet will have all the signs of good health, including a glossy coat, high energy, and bright eyes.

WHEN TO FEED

Start off with light, frequent meals because your puppy's stomach is so small. If the breeder has included a feeding schedule with your diet sheet, follow that as closely as possible and make increases or decreases as recommended. If no feeding schedule accompanied your puppy, set one up right away.

A four-month-old (or younger) Cavalier King Charles Spaniel should be fed four times a day. At four to six months of age, you can reduce the feedings to three, and after six months, you can start feeding once or twice a day, depending on your schedule. You should always feed him at the same time of day, starting out with breakfast, lunch, mid-afternoon snack, and dinner, which should be served an hour before bedtime. Take your puppy outside to go potty as soon as he is finished with his meal.

Some people recommend "free feeding" their dog, which means leaving food out for him to nibble on all day. This makes it harder to judge exactly how much the dog has eaten and makes it harder to predict when the dog needs to go outside to eliminate. It also could lead to overeating, because many Cavalier King Charles Spaniels will eat out of boredom. It is best to put the food down for your puppy for a limited time and then take the food away when the time is up. Your dog will adjust quickly to the schedule, and you'll have more control over the amount consumed.

HOW MUCH TO FEED

If you don't know the puppy's prior feeding schedule, you will have to figure out how much to feed him. Start off by following the directions on the dog food label and increasing or decreasing the amount as needed.

Providing treats in between meals will help prevent your Cavalier pup from overeating. Just remember that these treats are part of his overall caloric intake, so make them healthy.

Give the recommended amount for your puppy's age and take it away after a period of time. If your dog eats the food quickly and leaves nothing, you need to increase the amount. If there is leftover food, you may have to decrease the amount or feed him smaller meals more frequently.

TREATS

Treats are a great way to encourage and reward your Cavalier King Charles Spaniel for doing something well. There are plenty of treats avail-able today that are not only tasty, but also nutritious and beneficial to you dog's health. For example, hard biscuits can help keep his teeth clean. Remember to consider treats as part of your dog's total food intake. Limit the amount of treats you give your puppy, and be sure to feed him only healthy snacks. Avoid giving him table scraps, as they usually just add to his caloric intake. Obesity is a very serious health problem in dogs, so be sure to start your puppy off eating right.

BONES

Bones can help your puppy with his overwhelming need to chew. They keep his teeth clean and prevent him from becoming bored. Make sure you give your dog safe bones and toys made specifically for dogs, especially those that will not splinter or break into tiny pieces. Unfortunately, pieces might be swallowed and become stuck in your puppy's intestinal tract or cause him to choke. There are plenty of manufacturers that make safe, chewable, and edible dog bones, so give your Cavalier King Charles Spaniel something fun and safe to play with as a special treat.

SUPPLEMENTS

Healthy puppies that are fed a balanced diet will not need supplementation. In fact, some veterinarians believe that supplementing a puppy's diet with extra vitamins and minerals could aggravate certain conditions like hip dysplasia and hereditary skin problems. The only time you should give your puppy any kind of supplements would be under the direction of your veterinarian, and even then you should never exceed the prescribed amount.

Grooming Your Cavalier King Charles Spaniel

One of the Cavalier King Charles Spaniel's most attractive and distinguishing features is his beautiful silky coat. To keep it in prime condition, he will require daily grooming. Grooming is also important because it gives you a chance to inspect your dog and catch any skin or health problems before they start.

Puppyhood is the best time to begin grooming procedures. Your dog will become easily used to the grooming routine and soon come to expect it as part of everyday life. It is best to invest in a good grooming table if you plan to show your Cavalier King Charles Spaniel. While he is getting beautiful, your dog's leash can be attached to the grooming arm on the table, which will help keep him secure. Most tables have non-skid pads on the surface to keep him from sliding around. A grooming table will save your back as well, because it can be adjusted to your height and prevent you from having to bend over or kneel down.

Introduce your Cavalier King Charles Spaniel puppy to the grooming table slowly. Place the pup up there a few times without doing anything to him and give him a treat when you let him down. After you do this a few times, your puppy should eagerly get up on the grooming table. Then you can start lightly brushing him and running any appliances like hair dryers or clippers before actually doing any major grooming. When the dog appears totally comfortable, you can start grooming him on a regular basis. This gradual introduction will ensure that your puppy grows to enjoy his grooming time with you.

Once your puppy is accustomed to being touched, patted, and fussed over, you can begin a grooming routine that will keep him looking clean and healthy.

BRUSHING

Brushing your Cavalier King Charles Spaniel on a daily basis will go a long way toward maintaining his good looks. Daily brushing will reduce shedding, keep mats to a minimum, and allow you to inspect the coat for any foreign debris or skin problems. It also stimulates your dog's skin and spreads the coat's natural oils, which help keep a coat shiny and the skin healthy. Brushing on a routine basis means your dog will need to be bathed less often, because most of the dirt and debris in his coat will be removed regularly. The show Cavalier is not trimmed in any fashion, so regular brushing helps to keep that long, silky coat in tip-top shape.

Most dogs will thoroughly enjoy the time spent getting pampered by you every day. What puppy can resist lounging on his owner's lap while being brushed—it's a canine paradise!

BATHING

Most Cavalier King Charles Spaniels will require a bath only occasionally. Healthy dogs usually excel at keeping themselves clean, and regular brushing should keep your puppy's coat in good shape. In fact, over-bathing your dog can cause dry skin and irritation, which, in turn, might lead to excess scratching or infections. However, every puppy, at some time or another, will roll in something particularly smelly or dirty and require a bath. When you do give your puppy a bath, steps should be taken to make it as painless as possible.

TOENAIL AND FOOT CARE

Your Cavalier King Charles Spaniel's feet really take a beating. They endure the pounding of all that energy and traverse the terrain of every place he explores—whether over rocks, cement, wood, snow, or grass, your pup's feet get there first and suffer the hardest.

Thus, it is important to take good care of your dog's paws. Always examine your dog's feet as part of his daily grooming, and also watch for soreness or blisters. If he shows any signs of soreness or favors a leg when walking, take him to the veterinarian immediately.

Nail trimming is something that your dog should get used to during puppyhood. The earlier your Cavalier King Charles Spaniel gets used to nail trimming, the easier your life will be at grooming time. Nail trimming is not only done for appearances, but is necessary for your puppy's health and comfort. It can be very difficult to get your puppy to sit still for this, which is why it is easier to start while the dog is young. Also, if your puppy has a scary or painful experience, you may not get

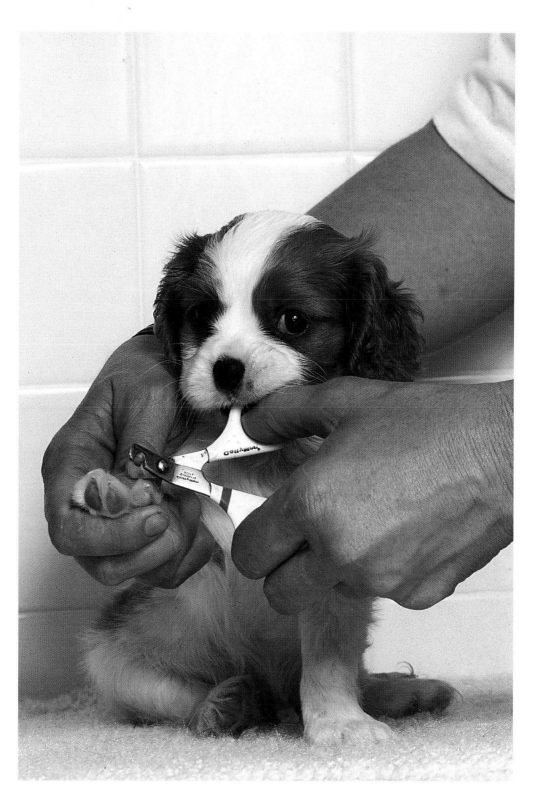

Your Cavalier's nails need to be trimmed on a regular basis. Use a nail clipper or a grinder to cut back the nail. Be careful not to cut into the quick, which will cause lots of pain for your dog.

a second chance, so try to make this procedure as comfortable and routine as possible.

Trimming your puppy's nails is not as hard as it may seem. The easiest way to do it is with a pair of canine nail clippers. You can also use an electric nail grinder if you find this method easier. Take care to avoid the quick, which is the area of the nail that contains nerves and blood vessels. If you accidentally cut the quick, it will bleed and cause your dog pain.

The Cavalier King Charles Spaniel has clear or white nails, so it is fairly easy to see the quick, which looks

Keep your Cavalier's ears clean at all times. Use a cotton swab or a damp cloth to wipe the ears clean.

like a pink line that extends from the base of the nail toward the tip. The best way to trim your puppy's nails is to be conservative and only snip a tiny amount at a time. Once you do it, repeating the procedure is easy for each nail, using the previous one as a model. If you do cut the quick, have a styptic pencil or powder on hand to curb the bleeding.

If trimming your Cavalier King Charles Spaniel's nails makes you too nervous—*don't ignore the task*. Go to an experienced groomer and let her do it for you. If you start now and add nail care to your weekly schedule, you and your puppy will be nail-trimming experts in no time.

EAR CARE

As in the case of any breed with hanging ears, the Cavalier's ears must be kept clean. Do not neglect your Cavalier King Charles Spaniel's ears when you groom him. Ear infections can be caused by excessive dirt, moisture, and bacteria in the ear canal. Dogs with long, floppy ears, like the Cavalier King Charles Spaniel, are especially prone to ear problems because their ear shape prevents adequate air circulation.

When taking care of your Cavalier King Charles Spaniel's ears, the first thing you should do is pluck or trim out (with blunt-nosed scissors) the excess hair. To maintain cleanliness, take a cotton ball or washcloth

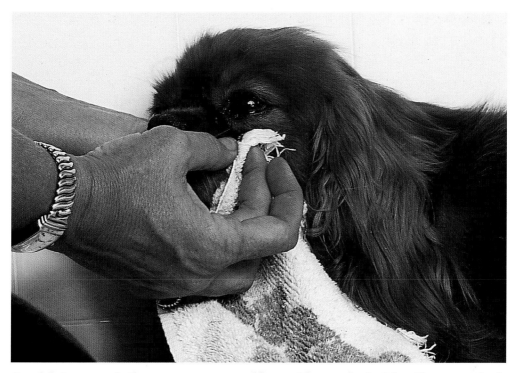

Any debris near or in the eyes can cause problems with your dog's vision. Keep your dog's eyes clean by wiping away any dirt that may be present.

dampened with commercial ear cleaner or mineral oil and wipe the inside of the earflap. If your dog's ear is sore, contains excess wax, or has an objectionable odor, he probably has an ear infection and needs to see the veterinarian immediately.

EYE CARE

It is fairly easy to keep your puppy's eyes clear, sparkling, and bright. First, make sure that you keep all debris, including hair, out of his eyes. Wipe them on a regular basis with a cotton ball or washcloth dipped in warm water. If your puppy's eyes appear red, cloudy, swollen, or have excess tearing, contact your veterinarian.

DENTAL CARE

Mitral valve heart disease seems to be somehow correlated with unhealthy teeth and gums. That's why it is especially imperative that you keep your Cavalier's teeth clean. If you do not brush your Cavalier King Charles Spaniel's teeth on a regular basis, plaque builds up on the teeth and under the gums. If this plaque is not removed, periodontal disease, a bacterial infection, can occur. If left untreated, the bacteria can enter the bloodstream and spread to your puppy's vital organs. Problems such as mouth abscesses and tooth loss may develop as well. Dogs that don't receive good dental care can even suffer from really bad breath, a feature

Provide your Cavalier with plenty of chew toys, such as those made by Nylabone®. They will keep him occupied and help keep his teeth clean at the same time.

that does not endear them to humans.

It is much easier to brush your puppy's teeth than you may think, as long as you have the right supplies. You should purchase a dog toothbrush or a finger toothbrush (a rubber cap that fits over your index finger) and toothpaste made for dogs. Never use human toothpaste when brushing your puppy's teeth. Dogs will not spit out the toothpaste, which can cause stomach upset and digestive problems. Also, the minty taste that humans enjoy probably will not appeal to your puppy as it does to you. Canine toothpaste are edible and come in "doggy-friendly" fla-

vors, such as beef and poultry, and are edible.

Chew Toys and Healthy Teeth

Your Cavalier, like all dogs, needs to chew. Chewing is a normal activity and helps to strengthen your dog's teeth. Many chew toys are designed to help clean your dog's teeth as he chews. The Nylabone® Dental Chew has raised tips that rub against the teeth and help to remove plaque. Another veterinarian-recommended product is Nylabone® Dental Chew Floss®, which cleans between the teeth as your dog chews. No matter which chew toys you choose, make sure they are safe for your dog.

Training Your Cavalier King Charles Spaniel

When you added a Cavalier to your family, you probably wanted a companion and a friend. You may have wanted a dog to go for walks, take jogs, or play with your children. To do any of these things, your puppy will need training.

Your new Cavalier King Charles Spaniel should be trained to eliminate outside; however, placing newspaper on the floor will make it easier to clean up any accidents.

Good basic training will transform your jumpy, squirmy, wiggly little puppy into a well-mannered Cavalier that is a joy to be around. A trained puppy won't jump up on people, dash out the open door, or raid the trash can. He will be able to be all you want him to be. However, your puppy needs to have someone tell him what to do. Your Cavalier has the right to be trained—it is unfair to leave him to figure out the human world on his own, and he won't be able to do it.

You, too, will benefit from training, because you will learn how to motivate your dog, prevent problem behavior, and correct mistakes that do occur. Puppy training entails much more than learning the traditional sit, down, stay, and come commands—it means that you will be teaching your puppy to live in your house. You can set some rules and expect him to follow them.

HOUSEHOLD RULES

Start teaching your puppy the household rules as soon as possible—preferably as soon as you get him home. Your eight- to ten-week-old puppy is not too young to learn what you expect of him. When you teach him these rules from the start, you can prevent bad habits from forming.

When deciding what rules you want him to follow, picture your puppy as the adult dog you want him to be. It may be cute to let your little Cavalier sleep on your bed every night, but are you going to want a bedmate a year from now? Take a practical look at your puppy and your environment and decide what behavior you can or cannot live with. It is important to make these decisions early in your dog's life, because what he learns as a puppy will remain with the adult dog.

HOUSETRAINING

One of the first things that you will undertake will be housetraining your Cavalier. You are teaching your dog that he has a specific place where he should eliminate—preferably outside. Your best bet is to start housetraining him as soon as possible. However, you need to remember that puppies between the ages of 8 and 16 weeks do not have control of their bladders or bowels. They are not able to "hold it" until they get a little older, which means that in the beginning, housetraining will take vigilance on your part. You will have to watch very carefully for signs that your puppy needs to eliminate. He will usually have to go to the bathroom after eating, drinking, sleeping, and playing. Most puppies will also give off signals, like circling or sniffing the floor. These behaviors are a sure sign that your puppy needs to go outside. When you see him display this behavior, don't hesitate. Carry your pup outside to the spot where you want him to eliminate. Then, praise your dog for eliminating in the proper spot.

A crate makes a great home for your Cavalier. When setting up the crate, such as this Nylabone® Fold-Away Pet Carrier, make sure you provide a comfortable blanket and several chew toys to make your dog at home.

CRATE TRAINING

With the help of a regular schedule, you will be able to predict the times that your puppy will need to potty. The most useful item that you can buy for your puppy to help facilitate this process is a crate. Nylabone® makes a Fold-Away Pet Carrier that folds up for easy storage when not in use. Training your puppy to use a crate is the quickest and easiest way to housetrain him. Remember that your Cavalier will be developing habits throughout this training period that will last him his lifetime—make sure you teach the right ones.

By about five weeks of age, most puppies are starting to move away from their mothers and littermates to relieve themselves. This instinct to keep the bed clean is the basis of crate training. Crates work well because puppies do not want to soil where they eat and sleep. They also like to curl up in small dark places that offer them protection on three sides, because a shield makes them feel more secure. When you provide your puppy with a crate, you are giving him his very own "den"—to your puppy's inner wolf, it is home sweet home. Pups will do their best to eliminate away from their den, and later, outside of the house.

Being confined in a crate will help a puppy develop better bowel and bladder control. When confined for gradually extended periods of time, the dog will learn to avoid soiling his bed. It is your responsibility to give your dog plenty of time outside the crate and the house, or the training process will not be successful.

Sometimes puppies really just need to get away from it all. The hustle and bustle of a busy household can be overwhelming at times. There are periods when your puppy will become overstimulated and need to take a "time out" to calm down (especially if you have rambunctious kids around), and a crate will be invaluable at these times. It can also be used as your puppy's place of refuge, since if he's tired, hurt, or sick, he can retreat to his crate to sleep or hide. If he's overstimulated or excited, you can put him in his crate to calm down. Even when you are doing work around the house that doesn't allow you to constantly watch the puppy, you can put him into his crate until you are done painting the bathroom or the workmen have left. In short, crates are lifesavers for puppy owners. Eventually, the puppy will think that it is pretty cool, too.

You should feed your new pup in his crate so he becomes used to it being his own "private place." Make sure members of the household know not to disturb your new dog when he's in his home.

The Nylabone® Fold-Away Pet Carrier sets up and folds down easily to give your Cavalier the perfect home anywhere he goes.

INTRODUCING THE CRATE

Introduce your puppy to the crate very gradually. You want the puppy to feel like this is a pleasant place to be. Begin by opening the door and throwing one of your puppy's favorite treats inside. You may want to teach him a command, like "bedtime" or "crate" when the pup goes into the crate. Let your dog investigate the crate and come and go freely. Don't forget lots of praise. Next, offer a meal in the crate. Put the food dish inside and, after awhile, close the door behind him. Open the door when he's done eating. Keep this up until your puppy eats all of his meals in the crate.

Soon your puppy will become accustomed to going in and out of the crate for treats and meals. If you do not wish to continue feeding him in his crate, you can start feeding him elsewhere, but continue offering the dog a treat when he enters the crate. Start closing the door and leaving your puppy inside for a few minutes at a time. Gradually increase the amount of time your puppy spends in the crate. Always make sure that you offer him a treat and praise for going in. It is also a good idea to keep a few favorite toys inside the crate as well.

Crate Don'ts

Don't let your puppy out of the crate when he cries or scratches at the door. If you do, he will think that complaining will bring release every time. The best thing to do for a temper tantrum is to ignore the pup. Only open the door when the dog is quiet and has calmed down.

In addition, don't use the crate as punishment. If you use the crate when he does something bad, your dog will think of the crate as a bad place. Even if you want to get the pup out of the way, make sure that you offer him lots of praise for entering the crate and reward him with a treat or toy.

CRATE LOCATION

During the day, store your puppy's crate in a location that allows him easy access and permits him to be part of the family. The laundry room or backyard will make a dog feel isolated and unhappy, especially if he can hear people walking around. Position the crate anywhere the family usually congregates—the kitchen or family room is often the best place.

At night, especially when your puppy is still getting used to the crate, the ideal place might be in your bedroom, near your bed. Your close presence will create a feeling of security for the dog and make life easier for you as well. For example, if the pup needs to go outside during the night, you can let him out before he has an accident. Your dog will also feel comforted by the smell, sight, and sound of you, and will be less likely to feel frightened.

OUTSIDE SCHEDULE

As was mentioned before, puppies need time to develop bowel and bladder control. The best way to most accurately predict when your Cavalier needs to eliminate is to establish a routine that works well for both of you. If you make a daily schedule of eating, drinking, and outside time, you will notice your puppy's progress.

Every person and family will have a different routine—there is no one right schedule for everyone. Just make sure that you arrange times and duties that everyone can stick with. The schedule you set will have to work with your normal routine and lifestyle. Your first priority in the morning will be to get the puppy outdoors. Just how early this should occur will depend much more on your puppy than on you. Once your puppy comes to expect a morning walk, there will be no doubt in your mind when he needs to go out. You will also learn very quickly how to tell a puppy's "emergency" signals. Do not test the young puppy's ability for self-control. A vocal demand to be let out is confirmation that the house-training lesson is learned.

It is also important to limit your puppy's freedom inside the house and keep a careful eye on him at all times. Many puppies won't take the time to go outside to relieve themselves because they are afraid that they will miss something; after all, everything exciting happens in the house, as that's where all the family members usually are. Unfortunately, you may

Given the proper training, these little Cavalier pups will be able to alert you when they need to go outside to eliminate.

find your puppy sneaking off some-where—behind the sofa or to another room—to relieve himself. By limiting the puppy's freedom, you can prevent some of these mistakes. Close bed-room doors and put baby gates across hallways. If you can't supervise your dog, put him in the crate or outside in a secure area.

ACCIDENTS WILL HAPPEN

When housetraining your dog, remem-ber that if the puppy has an accident in the house, it is not his fault, it's yours. An accident means that the puppy was not supervised well enough or wasn't taken outside in time.

If you catch your dog in the act, don't yell or scold him. Simply say "No!" loudly, which should startle and stop him. Pick your pup up and go out-side to continue in the regular relief area. Praise your puppy for finishing outside. If you scold or punish him, you are teaching him that you think going potty is wrong. Your dog will become sneaky about it, and you will find puddles and piles in strange places. Don't concentrate on correc-tion; emphasize the praise for going potty in the right place.

If you find a little surprise left for you, do not yell at your puppy for it and never rub his nose in it. He will have no idea what you are talking about, and you'll only frighten him. Simply clean up the mess and be sure to keep a closer eye on him next time.

Housetraining is one of the most important gifts that you can teach your dog, because it allows him to live as one of the family. Every puppy will make mistakes, especially in the beginning. Do not worry—with the proper training and lots of patience, every dog can be housetrained.

BASIC TRAINING

Collar and Leash Training

Training a puppy to a collar and leash is very easy and something you can start doing at home without assistance. Place a soft nylon collar on the puppy. The pup will initially try to bite at it, but will soon forget it's there, and even more so if you play with him while he's wearing it. Some people leave their dog's collar on all of the time; others put it on only when they are taking the dog out. If it is to be left on, purchase a narrow or round one so it does not mark your dog's fur or become snagged on furniture.

Once the puppy learns to ignore his collar, you can attach the leash to it and let him pull it behind him for a few minutes every day. However, if the pup starts to chew at the leash, simply keep it slack and let him choose where to go. The idea is to let your dog become familiar with the feel of the leash, but not to become accustomed to chewing it. Repeat this exercise a couple of times a day for two days, and the pup will get used to the leash without feeling restrained.

Next, you can let the pup understand that the leash will restrict his movements. The first time this happens, your dog will either pull, buck, or just sit down. Immediately call the pup to you and give him lots of praise. Never tug on the leash or drag the puppy along the floor. This might cause him to associate his leash with negative consequences. After a few lessons, the puppy will have familiarized himself with the restrictive feeling, and you can start going in a direction opposite from the pup. Lure the puppy to your side with the promise of a treat, call the pup to you enthusiastically, and continue walking. When the puppy is walking happily on the leash, end the lesson with lots of praise. There is no rush for your puppy to learn leash training, so take as long as you need to make him feel comfortable.

BASIC COMMANDS

Although your puppy should attend puppy kindergarten, begin training as soon as he feels is comfortable in your home and knows his name. It is also very helpful to take the lessons that you learn together in kindergarten and practice them at home. Doing your homework together will not only reinforce what you learn in class, it will allow you to spend some quality one-on-one time with your pup.

There are two very important things to remember when training your

Your Cavalier should get used to wearing a collar and leash before beginning any training activities.

All training activities should be fun for both dog and owner. A loving kiss shows how much you love your dog.

puppy. First, train the puppy without any potential distractions. Second, keep all lessons very short. Eliminating distractions is important because your puppy's full attention is essential for the success of the lesson. This will not be possible if there are other people, other dogs, butterflies, or birds to play with. Also, always remember that puppies have very short attention spans. Even when the pup has grown into a young adult, the maximum training time should be about 20 minutes. However, you can give the puppy more than one lesson a day, with three being the recommended amount, each spaced well apart. If you train any longer, the puppy will most likely become bored, and you will have to end the session on a down note, which you should never do.

Before beginning a lesson, always play a little game so that the puppy's mind is active and he is more receptive to training. Likewise, always end lessons with play time for the pup, and always end training on a high note by praising the puppy. This positive reinforcement will really build his confidence.

The Come Command

The come command is possibly the most important command you can teach your puppy—it may even save your dog's life someday. Knowing that your dog will come to you immediately when you call him will ensure that you can trust him to return to you if there is any kind of danger nearby.

Teaching your puppy to come when called should always be a pleasant experience. However, you should never call your puppy in order to scold or yell at him or he will soon learn not to respond. When the pup comes to you, make sure to give him a lot of praise, petting, and, in the beginning, a treat. If he expects positive things when he reaches your side, you'll never have trouble persuading your dog to come to you.

Start with your puppy on a long lead about 20 feet in length. Have plenty of your puppy's favorite treats on hand. Walk the distance of the lead, and then crouch down and say, "Come." Make sure that you use a happy, excited tone of voice when you call the pup's name, and he should come to you enthusiastically. If he does not, use the long lead to pull him toward you, continuing to use the happy tone of voice. Give the dog lots of praise and a treat when he gets to you. Continue to use the long lead until your puppy is consistently obeying the come command.

The Sit Command

As with most basic commands, your puppy will learn the sit command in just a few lessons. One 15-minute lesson each day should do the trick in no time. Some trainers will advise you that you should not proceed to other commands until the previous one has been learned really well. However, a bright young pup is quite capable of handling more than one command per lesson and certainly per day. As time progresses, you will be repeating each command as a matter of routine before a new one is attempted. This method is employed so the puppy always begins, as well as ends, a lesson on a high note, having successfully completed a task.

When teaching the sit command, first find a treat that your dog really likes and hold it right by his nose, so that all his attention is focused on it. Raise the treat above his head and say, "Sit." Usually, the puppy will follow the treat and automatically sit. Reward him with the treat for being such a good dog and don't forget to praise him. After a while, the pup will begin to associate the word "sit" with the action. Most puppies will catch on very quickly. When your dog has reached a point where he is sitting consistently with the treat, take it away and just use praise as a reward.

Do not attempt to keep the pup in a sitting position for too long. Even a few seconds is a long time for a impatient, energetic puppy, and you do not want him to get bored with the lessons before they have even begun.

The Stay Command

The stay command should follow your sit lesson, but this directive can be very hard for puppies to understand. Remember that your dog wants nothing more than to be at your side, so staying in one place while you walk away will be difficult for him. You should only expect your dog to perform this command for a few seconds at first, and then gradually work up to longer periods of time.

When teaching the stay command, first face the puppy and say, "Sit." Now step backward, commanding, "Stay." It is also very helpful to use the hand signal for stay—place your hand straight out, palm toward the dog's nose. Let the pup remain in this position for only a few seconds before saying, "Come," and giving lots of praise and a treat. Once your dog gets the hang of it, repeat the command again, but step farther back. If the pup gets up and comes to you, simply return to the original position and begin again. As the pup starts to understand the command, you can move farther and farther back.

Once your puppy is staying reliably from a short distance, the next test is to walk away after placing the pup. This will mean your back is to the dog, which will tempt him to follow you. Keep an eye over your shoulder, and the minute the pup starts to move, spin around, say, "Stay," and start over from the original position.

As the weeks go by, you can increase the length of time the pup is left in the stay position, but two to three minutes is long enough for a puppy. If he drops into a down position and is clearly more comfortable, don't worry. In the beginning, staying put is good enough!

The Down Command

From the puppy's viewpoint, the down command is one of the most difficult to accept. This position is submissive in a wild pack situation. A timid dog will roll over, which is a natural gesture of submission. A bolder pup will want to get up and might back off, not wanting to submit. The dog will feel that he is about to be punished, which would occur with this position in a natural environment. Once your puppy comes to understand this is not the case and that there are rewards for obeying, he will accept this position without any problem.

There are two ways to teach the down command. Obviously, with a dog the size of a Cavalier King Charles Spaniel, it will be easier to teach the down if you are kneeling next to him. Have your dog sit and hold a treat in front of his nose. When his full attention is on the treat, start to lower the treat slowly to the ground, saying, "Down." The pup should follow the treat with his head. Bring it out slowly in front of him. If you are really lucky, your puppy will slide his legs forward and lie down by himself. Give him the treat and lots of praise for being such a good dog. If your dog won't lie down on his own (and most puppies

The sit command is one of the easiest commands that your Cavalier will learn.

The down is one of the more difficult lessons for your Cavalier King Charles Spaniel to learn. Patience and persistence will make it easier for your dog to learn.

won't), you can try this method: After the puppy is sitting and focused on the treat, take the front legs and gently sweep them forward, while at the same time saying, "Down." Then, quickly tell the dog how good he is, reward him with a treat, and make a lot of fuss. Repeat this exercise two or three times only during one training session. The pup will learn the down command over a few lessons.

The Heel Command

All dogs should be able to walk nicely on a leash without a tug-of-war with their owners. Teaching your puppy the heel command should follow leash training. Heeling is best done in a place where you have a wall or a fence to one side of you, because this barrier will restrict the puppy's movements so that you only have to contend with forward and backward situations. Again, it is better to conduct the lesson in private and not in a place where there will be many distractions.

A slip collar will not be necessary for your puppy, as you can just as effectively instruct with a flat, buckle one. The leash should be approximately 6 feet long. You can adjust the space between you, the puppy, and the wall so that your pet has only a small amount of room to move sideways. It is also very helpful to have a treat in your hand so that your dog will be focused on you and stay by your side.

When teaching the heel command, hold the leash in your right hand and pass it through your left. Show your dog the treat so he focuses on it. Start walking while luring the puppy to your side with the treat. Walk a few steps, then stop and give him the treat and praise. Then begin the process again. Soon your pup will realize that he receives a reward for staying by your side. If he pulls ahead or lags behind, simply stop and lure him back to you with the treat until he is focused again.

Once the lesson is learned and the dog heels reliably, you may change your pace from a slow walk to a quick one, and the puppy will learn to adjust to your gait. A slow walk is always difficult for most puppies, because they are usually anxious to be on the move. End the lesson when the pup is walking nicely beside you. Open the lesson with a few sit commands so that you're beginning with success and praise.

ADVANCED TRAINING

The Canine Good Citizen® Test

A reliable way to ensure that your Cavalier possesses the good manners he will need in life is to train for the Canine Good Citizen® test. The American Kennel Club (AKC) has developed this program to encourage all owners to properly train their dogs. It emphasizes responsible dog ownership and teaching a puppy good manners in the home and in the community. All dogs of any age, purebred or mixed breed, can take the Canine Good Citizen® test and earn a certificate from the AKC, as well as add the CGC® title to his name.

The dog must complete ten steps in order to pass and must prove that he is a dog any person would like to own. In fact, the dog must demonstrate that he is safe with children, and would be welcomed as a neighbor.

Training your Cavalier for the Canine Good Citizen® test will make him welcome everywhere he goes.

An increasing number of states have now passed Canine Good Citizen® legislation, and the CGC® program has been adopted by several other countries.

The American Kennel Club encourages all dog owners to participate in this program, and you can find out where a test is being given in your area by contacting your local breed club or the AKC directly.

Therapy Dogs

There is nothing more rewarding than seeing someone else get as much happiness and delight out of your puppy as you do, and there are some dogs that just seem to love getting a smile out of anyone and everyone. Becoming involved with therapy work is a wonderful way to spread the joy of dog ownership to those who may most benefit from it. Statistics show that this aspect of health care is making a real impact and creating some remarkable results with the sick, the elderly, and people with special needs. If your Cavalier King Charles has a particularly even and friendly temperament, therapy work may be perfect for him and especially rewarding for you.

You might have your dog visit the elderly in nursing home or patients in hospitals, or enroll him in a program that helps educate children about the care and training of dogs. If you contact the following therapy programs or your local humane society, you will be better informed of programs in your area and the best way to get your puppy started. When your puppy becomes a therapy dog, he is doing more than enriching your life—he is making a valuable contribution to the quality of life of others.

Your Healthy Cavalier King Charles Spaniel

The Cavalier King Charles Spaniel is a basically healthy, sturdy, small dog with few but important health concerns. The most serious health problem is mitral valve disease (MVD). This is a problem with the left or mitral valve of the heart.

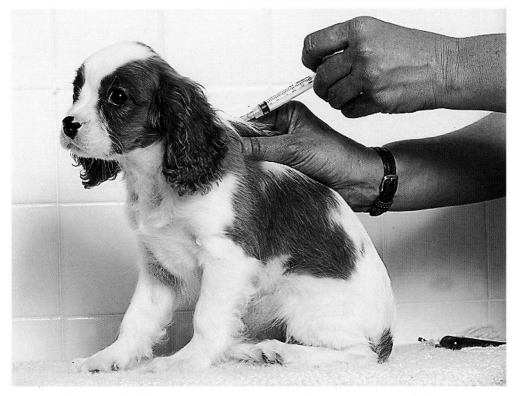

Your Cavalier King Charles Spaniel needs to receive his vaccinations to help protect him from certain illnesses. Contact your veterinarian to set up an inoculation schedule.

In this disease, the valve can thicken and degenerate, leading to congestive heart failure and, eventually, death. Although MVD is common in most toy breeds, it is of particular concern in Cavaliers because the disease may have an unusually early onset with a more rapid progression of symptoms as compared to other breeds. MVD has been found in all bloodlines and in Cavaliers from all countries, although conscientious breeders all over the world regularly check the health of their breeding stock for signs of early onset before breeding.

While Cavaliers do not commonly have serious eye problems, they can develop cataracts and other eye dis-

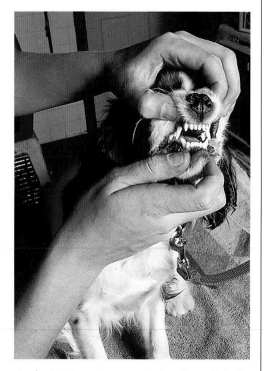

Annual visits to your veterinarian will help to keep your Cavalier healthy. Your vet can answer any questions that you may have about raising your pup.

eases. Careful breeders have certified veterinarian ophthalmologists check their breeding stock annually.

Another area of concern is luxating patellas (slipping kneecaps). This condition occurs when the knee lacks stability and can cause lameness. Luckily, Cavaliers with good bones and healthy parents are not generally candidates for this problem. Again, good breeding practices can curb these problems; be sure to discuss all of these conditions with your breeder when selecting a puppy.

PUPPY HEALTH

Every Cavalier King Charles Spaniel puppy should be vaccinated against the major canine diseases, including distemper, leptospirosis, hepatitis, and canine parvovirus. Your puppy may have received a temporary vaccination against distemper before you purchased him, but ask the breeder to be sure.

The age at which vaccinations are given can vary, but will usually occur when the pup is 8 to 12 weeks old. By this time, any protection given to the pup through antibodies received from his mother's initial milk will be diminishing.

The puppy's immune system works on the basis that his white blood cells engulf and render attacking bacteria harmless. However, these white blood cells must first recognize a potential enemy.

Vaccines are comprised of either dead or live bacteria in very small doses. Either type prompts the pup's defense system to attack them. When (and if) a substantial attack occurs, the immune system recognizes it and massive numbers of lymphocytes (white blood corpuscles) are mobilized to counter it. However, the ability of the cells to recognize these dangerous viruses can diminish over a period of time. It is therefore useful to provide annual defenses to protect against the enemy. This is done by means of booster injections that keep the immune system on alert. Immunization is not a 100 percent guaranteed success in preventing illness, but it comes very close. Certainly, immunization is better than giving the puppy no protection whatsoever.

Dogs are subject to other viral attacks. If there are high-risk factors in your area, your vet will suggest that you have the puppy vaccinated against these as well.

Your puppy or dog should also be vaccinated against the deadly rabies virus. In fact, it is illegal in many places for your dog not to be vaccinated. Immunization protects your dog, your family, and the rest of the animal population from this deadly virus that infects the nervous system and causes dementia and death.

PHYSICAL EXAMS

Your puppy should receive regular physical examinations or checkups. These come in two forms. One is obviously performed by your vet, and the other is a day-to-day procedure that you should carry out. Apart from the fact that these examinations will highlight any problem at an early stage, daily checkups are excellent ways to familiarize your puppy with handling.

To conduct the physical exam yourself, start at the head and work your way around the body. You should be looking for any sign of lesions or any indication of parasites on the pup. The most common parasites are fleas and ticks.

FIGHTING FLEAS

Fleas are very mobile and may appear red, black, or brown in color. Adults suck the blood of the host, while the larvae feed on the adults' feces, which are rich in blood. Flea "dirt" may be observed on the pup as very tiny clusters of blackish specks that look similar to freshly ground pepper. Flea eggs may be laid on the puppy, though they are more commonly laid off the host in a more favorable place, such as the bedding. They normally hatch in 4 to 21 days, depending on the temperature, but can survive for up to 18 months if temperature conditions are not favorable. The larvae are maggot-like and molt a few of times before forming a pupae, which can survive long periods until the temperature or the vibration of a nearby host causes them to emerge.

Regular grooming sessions will help to keep your Cavalier King Charles Spaniel looking his best. You can also examine your Cavalier for skin irritations or parasites that might be on him at this time.

There are a number of effective treatments available. Discuss them with your veterinarian, and then follow all instructions for the one that you choose. Any treatment will involve a product for your dog and one for the environment. This will require diligence on your part to treat all areas and thoroughly clean your home and yard until the infestation is eradicated.

THE TROUBLE WITH TICKS

Ticks are the arthropods of the spider family, which means they have eight legs (though the larvae have six). They bury their headparts into the host and gorge on its blood. Ticks appear as small, grain-like creatures sticking out from the skin. They are often picked up when dogs play in fields, but may also arrive in your yard via wild animals—even birds—or stray cats and dogs. Some ticks are species-specific; others are more adaptable and will host on many species.

The most troublesome type of tick is the deer tick, which spreads the deadly Lyme disease that can cripple a dog (or a person). Deer ticks are tiny and very hard to detect. Often, by the time they're big enough to notice, they've been feeding on the dog for a few days—long enough to do their damage. Lyme disease was named for the area in which it was first detected—Lyme, Connecticut—but has now been diagnosed in almost all parts of the US. Your veterinarian can advise you of the danger to the dogs in your area and may suggest your dog be vaccinated for Lyme. Always go over your dog with a fine-toothed flea comb when you come in from walking through any area that may harbor deer ticks. If your dog is acting unusually sluggish or sore, seek veterinary advice.

Attempts to pull a tick free will invariably leave the headpart in the pup, where it will die and produce an infected wound or abscess. The best way to remove ticks is to dab a strong saline solution, iodine, or alcohol on them. This will numb them, causing them to loosen their hold, at which time they can be removed with tweezers. The wound may then be cleaned and covered with an antiseptic ointment. If ticks are common in your area, consult with your vet for a suitable pesticide to be used in kennels, on bedding, and on the dog.

If your Cavalier King Charles Spaniel hunts often or spends a lot of time outdoors, you must be careful of other insects and outdoor dangers. Watch for many biting insects, such as mosquitoes, that can cause discomfort or transmit diseases to your Cavalier King Charles Spaniel.

A Cavalier King Charles Spaniel can easily get a grass seed or thorn lodged between his pads or in the folds of his ears. These may go unnoticed until an abscess forms. A daily check of your dog will do a world of good. If your puppy has been playing in long grass or places where there may be thorns, pine needles, wild animals, or parasites, the checkup is a wise precaution.

SKIN DISORDERS

Apart from problems associated with lesions created by biting pests, a puppy may fall victim to a number of other skin disorders, including ringworm, mange, and eczema. Ringworm is not caused by a worm, but rather is a fungal infection that manifests itself as a sore-looking bald circle. If your puppy has any form of bald patches, let your veterinarian check him over; a microscopic examination can confirm the condition. Iodine, carbolic acid, formalin, and other tinctures are older remedies for ringworm, but modern drugs are superior.

Proper care will keep your Cavalier King Charles Spaniel happy and healthy for many years to come.

Fungal infections can be very difficult to treat and even more difficult to eradicate due to the nature of the spores. These can withstand most treatments except burning, which is the best thing to do with bedding once the condition has been confirmed.

Mange is a general term that can be applied to many skin conditions in which the hair falls out and a flaky crust develops and falls away.

Often, dogs will scratch themselves, and this becomes invariably worse than the original condition, for it opens lesions that are then subject to viral, fungal, or parasitic attack. The cause of the problem is various species of mites. These either live on skin debris and the hair follicles, which they destroy, or they bury themselves just beneath the skin and feed on the tissue. Applying general remedies from pet stores is not recommended because the type of mange must be identified before a specific treatment can be effective.

Eczema is another non-specific term applied to many skin disorders. The condition can be brought about in many ways. Sunburn, chemicals, allergies to foods, drugs, and pollens, and even stress can all produce a deterioration of the skin and coat. Given the range of causal factors, treatment may be difficult because the problem is one of identification. Each possibility must be examined in order to correctly diagnose the matter. If the cause is dietary in nature, you must remove one item at a time in order to find out if the dog is allergic to a given food. The skin disorder could, of course, be the result of a nutrient deficiency, so if the condition persists, you should consult your veterinarian.

WORMS

Many species of worms exist, and a number of these live in the tissues of dogs and most other animals. Many present no problem at all, and so you will not even be aware they exist. Other worms can be tolerated in small levels, but become a major problem if they number more than a few. The most common types seen in dogs are roundworms and tapeworms. Roundworms represent the greater problem, while tapeworms require an intermediate host, so they are more easily eradicated.

Roundworms of the species *Toxocara canis* may grow to a length of 8 inches (20 cm) and look like strings of spaghetti. These worms feed on digesting food in a pup's intestines. In chronic cases, the puppy will vomit, have diarrhea, become pot-bellied, and eventually stop eating. Roundworms lay eggs in the puppy that pass out in his feces. They are then either ingested by the pup, or are eaten by mice, rats, or beetles. The puppy may then eat these and the life cycle is complete.

Larval worms can migrate to the womb of a pregnant bitch, or to her mammary glands, meaning they will be

A properly trained Cavalier is less likely to get into an accident. However, if he does, contact your vet immediately.

transferred to the puppy. However, the pregnant bitch can be wormed, which will help. The pups can, and should, be wormed when they are about two weeks old. Repeat the procedure every 10 to 14 days, and the parasites should be removed. Worms can be extremely dangerous to puppies, so make sure the pup is wormed as a matter of routine.

Tapeworms are viewed as tiny, rice-like eggs sticking to the puppy or dog's anus. They are less destructive, but still undesirable. The eggs are eaten by mice, fleas, rabbits, and other animals that serve as intermediate hosts. They then develop into a larval stage and must be consumed by a dog in order to complete the chain. Your vet will supply a suitable remedy if tapeworms are suspected. The vet can also perform an egg count on the pup's feces under the microscope; this will indicate the extent of infestation.

Other worms, such as hookworms and whipworms are also bloodsuckers. These parasites will make a pup anemic, which can be determined if blood is visible in the feces. The vet may then confirm the presence of tapeworm. Cleanliness in all matters is the best preventative measure for all worms.

BLOAT (GASTRIC DILATATION)

This condition has proved fatal to many dogs, especially large and deep-chested breeds, such as the Rottweiler or the Great Dane. However, any dog can develop bloat. This disorder occurs when gases build up in the stomach, especially in the small intestine. Carbohydrates are fermented and release gases. Normally, these gases are released by belching or expulsion from the anus. If for any reason these exits become blocked (such as if the stomach twists due to physical exertion), the gases cannot escape and the stomach simply swells and places pressure on other organs, sometimes cutting off the blood supply to the heart or causing suffocation. Death may easily follow if the condition goes undetected.

The best preventative measure is not to feed large meals or exercise your puppy or dog immediately after he has eaten. Reduce the risk of flatulence by adding more fiber to your dog's diet, refrain from feeding him too many dry biscuits, and maybe even add activated charcoal tablets to the diet.

ACCIDENTS

All puppies will receive their share of bumps and bruises due to the rather energetic way they play. These will usually heal over a few days. Small cuts should be bathed with a suitable disinfectant and then smeared with an antiseptic ointment. If a cut looks more serious, stem the flow of blood with a towel or makeshift tourniquet, and rush the pup to the veterinarian. Never apply too much pressure to the wound, as it might restrict the flow of blood to the limb.

In the case of burns, you should apply cold water or an ice pack to the surface. In the event of a chemical burn, wash the agent away with copious amounts of water. Then, apply petroleum jelly or any vegetable oil to the burn. Trim away hair if need be. Next, wrap the dog in a blanket and rush him to the vet. The pup may go into shock, depending on the severity of the burn; this, in turn, will result in a lowered blood pressure, which is dangerous and the reason the pup must receive immediate veterinary attention.

If a broken limb is suspected, try to keep the animal as still as possible. Wrap your pup or dog in a blanket to restrict movement and get him to the veterinarian as soon as possible. Do not move the dog's head into a backward tilting position, as this might result in blood entering the lungs.

Also, do not allow your pup to jump up and down from heights, as this can cause considerable shock to the joints. Like all youngsters, puppies do not know when enough is enough, so you must do all of their thinking for them.

Provided you strictly monitor your puppy's hygiene and check his physical state daily, you have done as much as you can to safeguard him during his most vulnerable period. Routine visits to your veterinarian are also recommended, especially while the puppy is under one year of age. The vet may notice something that you may have overlooked.

Resources

American Cavalier King Charles Spaniel Club, Inc.
Corresponding Secretary:
    Jacqueline Farrell
501 Williamsport
League City, TX 77573
Website: www.ACKCSC.org
Email: jackie@pfarrell.net

The Cavalier King Charles Spaniel Club (UK)
Secretary: Mrs. Annette Jones
Email: timsar.CKCS@btinternet.com

American Kennel Club
Headquarters:
260 Madison Avenue
New York, NY 10016

Operations Center:
5580 Centerview Drive
Raleigh, NC 27606-3390

Customer Services:
Phone: (919) 233-9767
Fax: (919) 816-3627
www.akc.org

The Kennel Club
1 Clarges Street
London
W1J 8AB
Phone: 087 0606 6750
Fax: 020 7518 1058
www.the-kennel-club.org.uk

The Canadian Kennel Club
89 Skyway Avenue
Suite 100
Etobicoke, Ontario, Canada
M9W 6R4
Order Desk & Membership: 1-800-250-8040
Fax: (416) 675-6506
www.ckc.ca

The United Kennel Club, Inc.
100 E. Kilgore Road
Kalamazoo, MI 49002-5584
(616) 343-9020
www.ukcdogs.com

Index